Wealth Shaman

Attracting Wealth Through Shamanic Principles

By

Michael William Denney

Disclaimer

Shamanism is an ancient way of living that teaches harmony. Shamanic techniques are powerful psychological and spiritual tools for solving problems. While the techniques shared in this book are powerful and proven, they are not a substitute for common sense. This book makes no guarantees or promises of any kind. Shamanic practices should never be considered as substitutes for psychological or psychiatric methods. It is assumed that the reader is relatively mentally and emotionally healthy. Those who suffer from serious psychological or emotional challenges should seek out professional help. Shamanic practices are not recommended for those who need professional counseling. In cases of serious emotional challenges, shamanism should only be practiced after receiving qualified psychological treatment.

Preface

Are you a spiritually inclined person who is conflicted when it comes to money?

Do the "normal" ways of obtaining wealth conflict with your personal or spiritual values? Do you feel spiritually drained working conventional jobs like sales, office jobs, food service, long hours of labor, etc?. . Do you struggle with ethical conflicts concerning Earth Friendly products and vocations? As a result, do you struggle to make ends meet because earning money the "normal" way by doing jobs that are harmful to your spirit keep you from earning a comfortable living? Or do you feel guilty when you do make money by promoting a company or product that harms the environment but there seems to be no other way to earn money?

Have you tried to make a living through Spirit Friendly ways, but have gotten nowhere because modern society doesn't seem to understand what you offer to the world?

In ancient times, tribal cultures that lived in harmony with Nature celebrated and honored their shamans. Spiritual leaders were materially supported by their community. People sought them out for their uniqueness and made sure their spiritual servants were well cared for. But in today's modern society, spiritually sensitive people are usually overlooked and are forced to work jobs that are destructive to their sensitive natures. This can lead to depression and financial self-sabotage.

There is a way to celebrate your spiritual uniqueness and make a good living. I'm NOT talking about a re-hashed version of "The Secret" or some other New Age gimmick like subliminal CD's, self hypnosis, life coaching or positive affirmations. I'm talking about ancient shamanic principles of living that can create abundant prosperity and allow you to be spiritually fulfilled expressing your true spiritual gifts.

Introduction

I struggled with my spiritual calling for much of my adult life. I have always been very creative, sensitive and shy. Although I was called to be a shaman early in life, I didn't understand it. My natural spiritual gifts made me feel different and weird. I thought that I was just strange and didn't fit in. My sensitivity made others uncomfortable so I hid my shamanic abilities. Instead, I focused on my artistic abilities. (Which is just another form of shamanism ☺) My plan was to make a living in the arts. But making a living in the arts in modern society is very difficult. Not every talented artist, singer, musician or actor can make a good living sharing his/her creative talents with the world. I found I was forced to do the "nine to five" thing every day just to keep a roof over my head and food in my stomach. As a shaman, I am naturally good with people so as a result, I made good money in sales. I used my inherent ability to "read" people to know how to close the sale. Closing sales was part of my job and I never lied to anyone. So, I wasn't doing anything wrong. But I felt like I was not living up to my true potential. I was slowly dying inside. I would look outside the window of my cubicle and see the sunlight and blue sky and wish I could be out in the fresh air at the beach or in the mountains. Every day after work, I would come home and think about how I had spent my day inside an office and compare it with the idea of just being out in nature and no matter how much money I had made that day, I would feel an emptiness inside. I felt like I had wasted the whole day and damaged my spirit. According to my shamanic values, spending the whole day outside surfing was actually accomplishing something. It felt real. While inside the office, I felt that I was wasting my precious time accomplishing nothing. I was only there to make money so I could survuve. On the surface, I appeared successful because of the money I was earning, but internally, I was unfulfilled because I knew I was not living my original spiritual destiny. But what else could I do? The modern world only respects money. And if I wanted the respect of my family and peers and be able to survive I had to do what everyone else was doing…Right? Wrong!

My life is much different now. I live in a comfortable home. I have everything I need on a physical level. I practice my shamanic calling. I have plenty of free time, a beautiful, loving marriage. I live near Nature and spend lots of time in the outdoors. I play music, and teach classes in spiritual living. In short, I am living my dream and following my spiritual calling. What did I do differently? Well, after a while I was simply unable to make a living doing the "normal" thing. No matter how hard I tried, I could not seem to close those sales anymore. I was utterly miserable. I was in the process of trying to create a business when the rug was pulled out from beneath me and I was forced to abandon my latest business scheme. I was 39 years old with no money, no relationship and no future prospects. I did not know what to do. I was very scared. I went for a walk and tried to figure out my next step. No matter how I looked at it, I could not see any way out of my current dilemma. I wanted to run away. So, I started fantasizing about where I would run to and what I would do. I found myself saying, "If I could do anything I wanted, where would I go and what would I do?" I began creating this fantasy of my new imaginary life. After about 10 minutes of fantasizing I decided to come back to "reality." I was very sad about leaving this fantasy I had created. I said out loud, "If I could do anything I wanted... WAIT! I CAN do anything I want. There is nothing stopping me except for me." What I had done by "fantasizing" about running away was to tap into my true desires for how I wanted to live my life. I thought that it was not possible because I had put limitations on what I was "supposed" to do and be. But I realized that I was holding on to other peoples' ideas about what I was "supposed" to do. Once I saw that my "fantasy" was my true desire and calling, I instantly decided I was going to move away and immediately create my new fantasy life. I gave notice to my job, said goodbye to my business partner, said goodbye to my friends, packed up my stuff and headed out to my new life in a different part of the country. Within a couple weeks, before I had even left town, I had met my future wife. She was living in the area I was moving to. I went out to visit her, made contacts in that city and began setting up new work for myself in the exact areas I had "fantasized" about. Now this may be an extreme example. You may not be able to simply leave everything behind and move to another part of the country as I did. But, the same principle still applies. By using shamanic techniques you will be able to contact the spirit of your ideal life and call it into existence. We are going to examine what you REALLY want to do and we will bring it into existence for you. We will not have to *make* it happen, we will simply call it to us. But, I warn you. Your ideal life may be very different from what you think. You may have to change your idea of who you are. So, keep an open mind and just allow yourself to go on an adventure...

What is a Shaman?

Shamanism is the practice of communicating and balancing the external world by means of spirit communication. A Shaman acts as a mediator between the spiritual and physical realms. The Shaman is like a human ambassador to the spirit realm. Average people seek out shamans because they themselves are unable or are not comfortable communicating with the spirit realm. So, they seek out shamans to interpret the energetic message of the world around them. Everything has a spirit, Rocks, Trees, Water, people, animals, ideas, things. Everything has its own spirit and we can communicate directly with them. Spirits communicate with us all the time. We have just chosen not to listen. Since everything has a spirit, everything can be communicated with. The shaman communicates directly with the spirit of whatever they wish to understand. In this book we will learn how to communicate with the spirit of our poverty and transform it into our prosperity. We will also learn how to determine our true purpose in life and follow it.

This is not a book on how to become filthy rich by selling real estate, buying stocks, internet marketing or online auctions. This is not another version of "The Secret." In fact, I am not going to tell you what you should do at all. In this book, we will examine what is missing from the "Law of Attraction" and why it doesn't work.
I am going to help you learn how to listen to your highest destiny and follow it. We are moving into a new age. In this new era, in order to be successful and enjoy life, humans will need to follow their highest spiritual calling in order to be supported materially by the Universe. In this new era, those who resist their innermost spirits will be frustrated. In the past, people were rewarded for resisting their spiritual paths and rewarded for following empty materialism. Those days are coming to an end. How many famous movie stars have we seen in recent times completely destroy their lives? All their fame and money could not buy them fulfillment. So, we are seeking a new paradigm about wealth. It is a new paradigm to us but, as we will see, it is as old as the hills.

What is Shamanic Wealth?

True wealth according to shamanic principles is being supplied with all your physical needs like a nice home, transportation, food, friends, love and family. Wealth is not about how much money, fame or possessions you have. True Wealth is balanced. A truly wealthy person according to shamanic principles has more than enough money to provide for their physical well-being as well as their leisure activities. A true shaman is able to live comfortably, have plenty of leisure time, go on vacations and follow a spiritually fulfilling vocation whether that be in big business, the arts, politics, spiritual teaching or just being a stay at home parent. Whatever is your true calling, if you are in communication with your higher self, the Universe will provide you with abundant wealth. So, in order to obtain wealth we first need to understand some basic shamanic principles.

Shamanic Principles

1) Everything in the Universe wants to behave according to its original spirit.
2) When something acts contrary to its original spirit, this creates imbalance.
3) Imbalance is the cause of all illness and pain.
4) When anything is in a state of imbalance, the spirit of that person, thing or entity has become lost. This causes dis-ease or illness.
5) By re-directing energy to act in accordance with its original purpose, its spirit is "retrieved," balance is restored and the illness is cured.

If you are struggling with money issues, then we can deduce three things:

a) You are not acting in harmony with your original spirit and your spirit has become lost or angry resulting in a state of imbalance.
b) Your imbalance has created an illness of poverty.
c) By discovering your original purpose and acting in accordance with your original purpose, your original spirit will return and poverty can be transformed into prosperity.

This may sound oversimplified, but is not. Making this transformation may not be easy, but it is very simple...

Acceptance

The first thing we want to do is recognize that your poverty does exist. Denial will not solve anything. In fact, our poverty is a direct result of resistance and denial of our true spiritual purpose. Your poverty exists because of some imbalance in you that has manifested itself in the form of a lack of finances. This is a form of soul sickness and needs to be spiritually treated. Resistance to your original purpose has choked off the energetic flow of the Universe to you and resulted in the form of financial lack. By accepting that we are in a state of imbalance we can then make the changes necessary in order to re-open the spiritual valves and let the energy flow to us again, thereby bringing us back into balance and restoring our birthright of prosperity.

Each of us is born with a divine purpose that we must fulfill in order to be truly happy. When we are one with our original spirit, we intuitively act in accordance with our divine purpose. When someone is following their divine purpose, the Universe provides them with everything they need for their physical survival (which includes money.) They are personally fulfilled and happy. However, sometimes we are diverted from our original purpose by the advice of well-meaning family, friends, teachers, society, etc... We may come to believe that our original Divine purpose is somehow "wrong." In my case, I was called to be a creative person as well as a shaman. My family and much of the society I grew up with did not approve of either of those callings and in order to gain acceptance from family and friends, I resisted my internal desires. I am not alone in this. We often become conflicted within ourselves. Struggling through this conflict is strengthening to the spirit. But sometimes through guilt, manipulation, peer pressure, etc, we may choose to abandon our innermost dreams and we try to "fit in." In essence, when we do this, we "evict" our original spirit. It becomes angry and leaves us. But because we are conflicted and our spirit is angry, it hangs around outside of us and sabotages our financial success in order to get our attention. We may think it is just "bad luck" or bad circumstances or just laziness on our part. But it is actually our own spirit running around causing problems so we will remember our original purpose and act accordingly. When we do act according to our original purpose, we automatically invite our spirit back inside of us where it belongs. Then the energetic doors are open for us to receive all of the things we need for our physical and emotional wellbeing. This can be a very simple process, but sometimes it is also frightening and painful. In either case, if we are resolute and willing to face our fears, we can be successful.

When we realize that our poverty and our prosperity are living beings that we can communicate with, we can get to the core of our problem much faster just by communicating directly with them and finding out what they want from us. You can spend years trying to intellectually figure out the core issue of your "poverty consciousness" and get nowhere. This is because we waste our time *thinking* about our poverty when we can simply communicate directly with the poverty itself and find out why it is there.

Your poverty, like everything else in the Universe, has a spirit. So let's just talk to it and find out what it has to say...

Exercise One: Talking to Your Poverty

In this exercise, we are going to communicate directly with the spirit of our poverty. But we first need to create and find two important things, our "Safe Room" and our Spirit Guides.

Constructing your "Safe Room"

Before we do this exercise, we first need to create a "safe room." A safe room doesn't even have to be a room. It can be outdoors in a meadow, a garden, a beach, a mountaintop… wherever. It can also be indoors like a temple or a courtyard. It can be whatever you want. You are going to build it. And you can build anything you want or go anywhere you want. For now, I will call it a safe room because it is a place of complete safety. You can meet and talk with anything and anyone and you will be completely protected. Even if you call in a dangerous animal or even the devil himself, he cannot harm you in your safe room because you will be completely protected by Divine Spirit.

In your safe room, you are going to invite your poverty to come and meet with you face to face to ask it why it is in your life and what you need to do to transform it into prosperity. But first we need to bring your spiritual protector to guide you and protect you. So, let's build your safe room.

If you are new shamanic work, you may want to find a private place to do your shamanic exercises. If you are experienced in meditative or shamanic practices, you will be able to do this almost anywhere. For now, I will assume you are a novice in shamanic thinking.
So, find a quiet spot. It can be anywhere indoors or outdoors. Get comfortable and relax. I am going to teach you a shamanic breath which will enable you to access an altered, energetic state of consciousness. It is the 3-1-3-1 breath. First make sure you are breathing deeply from your abdomen. Now, Inhale deeply to a count of 3, then hold for a count of 1, exhale for a count of 3 and hold for a count of 1. Repeat. Continue like this for 3 minutes or for as long as you like. When you feel yourself enter an altered state of consciousness, you are now able to contact other dimensions.

Building Your Room

When you have achieved a mildly altered state of consciousness, you can begin building your safe room. For now, close your eyes and allow yourself to imagine some place that makes you feel comfortable and happy. One good way to do this is to ask yourself this question. "Where do I want to be right now?" say it out loud and then watch what happens. Often times people think they know what they want. By asking yourself the question, your subconscious will begin creating what you want on a very deep level. So ask the question and let the picture materialize in your mind. It may be different than what you expect. But you will find that it is deeply relaxing for you. When you have the basic outline of your room or garden or mountaintop or whatever, now you can add little touches if you choose. Decorate your room however you'd like. Or maybe it is just fine the way it is. When you are comfortable with your room, you may end the journey. To do this, you can say something like, "I consecrate this (Mountain, room, temple etc...) as my private sacred space. This sacred space will be available to me whenever I call you." Now, you have instructed the energy pattern of that safe space to remain in the spirit realm and manifest for you whenever you call it. Now, you can come back to it anytime you want.

Contacting Your Spirit Guide

Now that we have created your safe room, we can now contact your spirit protectors or spirit guides. You may not know it, but you already have many spirit protectors and guides. They have been sent to you by Spirit to help and guide you throughout your life. They are very humble and have been strictly instructed not to interfere with your free will. They are only allowed to intervene if you are in extreme danger of not fulfilling some very crucial aspect of your Life Purpose. The rest of the time, they simply stand to the side until you ask for their help. But, until you ask, they will give you your privacy.

If you know your spirit guides, then great. If not, then we will contact them together and invite them to come with us into your safe room.

Inviting Your Guides Into The Safe Room

First, do the 3-1-3-1 breath for a few minutes or until you feel deeply relaxed. Now, close your eyes and allow yourself to go to your safe room. To help you, you can invite your guides into your safe room. To do this, you say out loud, " I welcome my guides into this sacred space." Then watch and see who shows up. It may be a person, angel, animal or spirit. Your guides may manifest in whatever form they feel is most helpful for you. If however one of your guides is in a form that you are not comfortable with, ask them to change into a shape that you can communicate with better. This will usually result in a mutually acceptable situation for both of you. Next simply ask your guides to help and protect you in your safe room. At this point, you can ask your guides any question or listen if they choose to speak to you. It is also OK to say nothing and just allow their spiritual presence strengthen you.

Communicating To Your Poverty

Now we are going to invite your poverty into your safe room. Go through the previous outlined steps of breathing, going to your safe room and inviting your guides to be with you. When you have established that, then place a chair in the middle of your safe room. This is where your poverty is going to sit. You will be safe and your guides and protectors are there. Now say, "I invite my poverty to come sit in this chair in my safe room (or meadow, beach, etc...) Now, allow your poverty to materialize in whatever form it chooses. It may be a shape, an animal, a person, a monster. The first time I did this exercise, my poverty manifested as a ball of spikey, angry flesh that sat and growled at me. After talking to it, I discovered that it wasn't really angry but lonely and scared. Your case may be different. It may be an uncomfortable sight. But, that's OK. You are safe. In whatever form your poverty chooses to manifest is OK because it is already with you anyway. What more harm can it do you? At least now you can see it for what it truly is and you are protected by your guides. It may not be frightening. It may be comical. It doesn't matter.

Now, ask your poverty, "Why are you here?" "What do you want?" "What can I learn from you about my original purpose?" These are some example questions. Create your own questions if you like, but these work well. Take time between each question to listen to the answers. Now tell your poverty that you accept that it is in your life now and your goal in these sessions is to find out how you can transform your poverty into prosperity. Ask your poverty to work with you to find a solution to your financial issues. You can even ask your poverty for a truce by assuring your poverty that you are committing to examine how you are out of balance with your true purpose. You may find that if your poverty is angry, it will calm down considerably and be more co-operative. When you are done with your session, immediately go write down what your poverty told you. This will be helpful to you later.

Exercise One: Analysis

Hopefully, now you have some good insights from your session speaking to your poverty. Based on my experience, it is possible that you saw, heard and experienced some things you weren't expecting. Possibly some things were strange or confusing. That's OK. The things that might seem confusing will most likely be the most profound for you. So, I want to share a secret with you that you might have already guessed or intuited from some of the things I have already said. The secret is this: Your Poverty is your Prosperity. Meaning - that thing that is designed to help you when you are operating from your highest destiny is also the same thing that will sabotage you when you are not acting from your original purpose. Make sense?

Let me give you an example. Often times, physical illness is not a result of invasive germs but from toxicity in the body. Symptoms of toxicity are often identical to viral or bacterial illness. Many times people seek a cure by suppressing uncomfortable symptoms. But in the long run, this can make the illness worse, because all they are doing is covering up the symptoms and not addressing the real cause of the toxic buildup. Stuffy nose, watery eyes, scratchy throat are simply the effects of the immune system warning you that there are toxins in the body. So, by suppressing the symptoms, all you are doing is sabotaging your body's warning system. So, in this case, by suppressing symptoms, the person is just fighting their own immune system and making themselves more sick. The shaman way is to listen to the immune system and ask it what it wants. By listening to the immune system's response, you can determine the true cause of the toxic buildup, remove the toxic source and cure yourself of the dis-ease.

The same principle applies to your poverty. Your poverty is merely your prosperity telling you that you are not in balance with your original life purpose. This is damaging to your spirit. So your prosperity needs to warn you that you are straying from the very thing that will bring you the most happiness. If you were allowed to get rich doing something that is less than fulfilling, your prosperity would be helping to harm you. And of course that would be antithetical to the shamanic meaning of prosperity. As I stated before; when you stray from your original purpose, you evict your prosperity from your life. Your prosperity is yours. It belongs with you and only you and when you kick it out, you hurt it's feelings and make it angry. How would you feel if your best friend, lover, etc... kicked you out of your only home? What if then you tried to find another home but you couldn't? You would now be homeless. Well, this is what happens when we stray from our true path. Our prosperity becomes homeless and wanders around for a while and then realizes that YOU are it's true home and so it tries to get your attention. If you don't listen to the first subtle hints, then your prosperity is forced to become your poverty to get your attention. The longer you stray from your original path, your prosperity (now your poverty) gets more and more angry and sabotages your finances more and more until you are forced to listen.

Another shamanic principle is this:
Your greatest weakness is your greatest strength
Your greatest strength is your greatest weakness

Exercise Two: Listening to Your Prosperity

So, this exercise will be easy since you now know that your poverty is really your prosperity inverted.

Go to a quiet place and prepare for your shamanic exercise. Do your breathing, travel to your safe room, invite your guides, set up the chair and invite your prosperity into the chair. When your prosperity arrives, take note of how it looks and feels. Now, the first thing you want to do is apologize to your prosperity. You can say something like, "I'm sorry for abandoning you. I did not realize that I was driving you away from me. I love you. Please forgive me." You may want to hug your prosperity or merge yourself with it again. But, like meeting an old friend you have been feuding with, you just want to heal the hurt in whatever way is best for both of you. After you have made-up and re-established an energetic connection, now ask your prosperity, " What do you want me to do?" How can I best follow my original spirit and have a healthy financial life?" Listen to what your prosperity tells you. You can make up your own questions and talk with your prosperity for as long as you want. When you are done with the exercise, be sure to write down what was said. I know you may think that you will remember what you heard, but, trust me, you may forget, so be sure to write it down. Writing it down also reinforces the messages and allows it to penetrate deeply into the spirit and brain...

Exercise Two: Analysis

It is possible that your prosperity has told you some things you did not understand or did not want to hear. This is normal. There is a reason why you have become separated from your original purpose. You have been resisting your original destiny out of some misplaced fear that you probably learned in your childhood. These psychological patterns are very deep and can be very frightening and painful to face. It is possible that when you asked your prosperity how you can have a healthy financial life, it may have told you to do something that seemingly has no connection with money. You may be wondering, "How can I make a living doing **that**? These may be the same kinds of things your parents, peers, teachers and friends told you when you first thought about doing these things. When I was in college, other students, (especially business majors) would ask me what my major was and I would say, "Humanities/classical languages." The first thing they would say in response was "What the hell're you gonna do with **that**?" Meaning, "How can you possibly make a living learning that nonsense?" We have become a society where a real education and critical thinking are not important unless it can translate into huge profits. This is part of the problem with modern society... But, I digress...

So whatever your prosperity told you that you needed to do is correct. You can trust it. You may need to meditate on the deeper meanings. You may not see how it can result in wealth right now, but if you trust it, it will bring you prosperity. The best advice I can give you is to do exactly what your prosperity told you to do. When you do this, you will send out energy vibrations into the fabric of the Universe that will reverberate back to you in the form of whatever you need to accomplish your purpose. (Which includes money) Whatever your prosperity told you that you needed to do is the very thing that will bring you the most happiness and success in your life. We must remember that from a spiritual perspective, money is the *result* of correct action, it is not the sole purpose of our lives. Because we are physical beings, we often try to address our physical needs first, then look at our spiritual needs. But this is actually backwards, especially for spiritually minded people and this is not the shamanic way.

If you are still worried and confused as to how you can make a living doing whatever your prosperity told you to do, then you can go back to your safe room and sit down with your prosperity and try to make a compromise... Now, I can't guarantee that your prosperity will listen. There have been times when I tried to compromise with my prosperity and the answer was "no." But you can try. One approach is to say something like, " I accept that doing _____ is my original destiny and I promise to begin doing that right now. But, please forgive me, I don't see how that will bring me money right now and I need something to pay bills this month. I am confused and I want to feel like I am doing something that will bring money in now. Is there something I can be doing right now that will bring me some money?" Like I said, the answer may be "no." But if you show that you are serious there may something you can come up with for the time being while you are implementing the big picture stuff.

But having read this last paragraph, it sounds like my own resistance being projected onto the page. So, it may be better to just simply do what your prosperity says and trust that the Universe will take care of you. When I think about it, this has always been the case for me. Regardless of how things may have looked, I have always gotten everything I needed at the time.

Creating A New Dream With Shamanic Fantasy

In the introduction I shared with you how fantasizing catapulted me into my new successful life. I stumbled onto this technique by accident and I am sure you do this all the time also. It is a very human habit to fantasize about our ideal lives. So, what is the difference between those who bring their fantasy into reality and those who simply fantasize about it and never bring it into external reality? You're probably expecting me to say something like, *"The difference is those who are living their fantasy worked really hard to make it happen."* That's what I have heard all my life. But guess what? That strategy has never worked for me. In fact, for me, the harder I try to *make* something happen, the faster it runs away from me. However, I have seen this kind of strategy work for others, but never for me. I think I know why. It is because I am born to be a shaman in this life. The average person runs toward their fantasy like a hunter and subdues it. A shaman works cooperatively with the spirit of things and calls them to him/herself. For the average person, this sounds like laziness. For the average person, shamanic techniques may be an ineffective strategy. Therefore judging shamanic fantasy as laziness is a very effective problem solving strategy for those people who are unfamiliar with it because it motivates them to work hard in the external realm to accomplish their goal (according to their nature.) I would argue therefore, that chasing after one's dreams in the external realm is laziness for the shaman, because it is an ineffective strategy for them. I have come to believe that there are different kinds of people in this world who are designed to operate with reality on different levels. Many people are best suited to work hard in the physical realm in order to bring ideas into external reality. Shamans are designed to work with the internal spiritual essence of things and are best suited to bring ideas into external reality by working in the energetic realm. Shamans are like birth facilitators. We help bring ideas and concepts into external reality by birthing them. Once they are in reality, then others can chase them down. As soon as I was able to accept that I was different from other people, I didn't need to try and be like them. Nor did I need to try and compare myself to them

In times past, every community had a shaman. If a child was born into that community who showed themselves to be different, this would be recognized by the community and the child would be presented to the tribal shaman to determine if the child was sick or was born to be a shaman. If the child was determined to be a shaman, then what was once seen as strange was now viewed as special. The tribe understood that the shaman had an ability to mediate on behalf of the tribe in the spiritual realm. It was expected that the shaman would operate in external reality in a different fashion than everyone else. The average person in the tribe may not understand the shaman or may even be a little frightened of them, but they all knew that the shaman was special and necessary for the tribe's survival. At this point, the tribal shaman would take the child under their tutelage to train them to be the next shaman of the tribe. Modern society has abandoned this practice. The result is that naturally born shamans are cast aside or worse yet, expected to function like the rest of society. Since shamans have not been recognized in modern society and have been expected to function like everyone else, many times, the shaman ends up simply being a misfit outcast, a dreamer. So, if you have been the type of person who has not been able to chase things down like everyone else. If you are sensitive and creative, you may be a shaman. It may be that instead of trying to do things the way others do, you can try to call things to you instead of hunt them down like most people do. In the next chapter, we will learn how to use fantasy as a tool to bring things into being into our external reality.

Exercise Three: Shamanic Fantasy

I don't need to teach you how to fantasize. I am sure you already know how to do that. What I am going to share with you is how to communicate with yourself during fantasizing so that instead of abandoning the fantasy afterward (like we are taught to do), you can empower the fantasy to take on a life of its own and continue to work for you after you have come "back to reality."

Warm -Up: No Rules...

So, here is the first step to your fantasy exercise... We are going to get warmed up for the real fantasy exercise here. This is not the real exercise. It is just a warm-up exercise just for fun to warm up our imagination. The goal of this warm-up is to free yourself from all unnecessary constraints. You will need a notebook and a comfortable space where you can be alone and relaxed. For some, that means going to a park or the beach. Sitting in a bathtub or a Jacuzzi works for others. For some, it is just having some alone time in your favorite chair at home. Make a time to do this. If you can do it right now, then go there now. Wherever it is for you, find 20 or 30 minutes and go there with your notebook. Put a bookmark in this book and stop reading this chapter until you are ready to finish this step.... Seriously... Stop reading and come back when you have 20 or 30 minutes to do this exercise...

OK... Hopefully you are now alone in your favorite secret relaxing spot where you will be undisturbed for some time. Now, here is the warm-up exercise... Get your notebook out and say these words out loud... *"If I had no obligations or restrictions of any kind and I could do anything I wanted and I mean ANYTHING at all no matter how silly or unrealistic it was... What would I do?"* OK, now write down the first fantasy that comes to mind....

Spend some time enjoying that fantasy knowing that it is just a warm-up exercise. Since this isn't the real fantasy that you are going to act on, you can go totally nuts and indulge in the most outrageous, unrealistic, childish fantasy. It doesn't have to be outrageous or unrealistic, but for the purposes of this warm-up exercise, feel free to be as unrealistic as possible. We are going to train our imaginations to think outside of the box, so it is important that you drop all "common sense" restrictions. Let go of all those responsible people in your head who would tell you that your fantasy is selfish or unrealistic or unproductive, etc... Do you fantasize about living in a hammock on a tropical beach living off of wild coconuts and spear fishing for your dinner every day? Don't scoff. I know a guy who did just that. Can you imagine looking back on six months of just living in nature and spear fishing? My friend lives with that memory because he did it. Whatever your totally unrealistic fantasy is, the only requirement is that it makes you deliriously happy. Now, write down this fantasy in detail and then spend 30 minutes seeing yourself living this fantasy. Close the book now and don't open it until you have written out your fantasy and allowed yourself to get completely lost in it.

Warm-Up -Analysis

OK, how was that? Did you have a good time? If you did not, close the book right now and go back and do it again until you find an irresponsible, childish fantasy that really is nothing but guilty fun and then come back to this chapter...

OK... Hopefully you have indulged yourself in a very fulfilling, but unrealistic fantasy. Now, we are almost ready to do the REAL exercise that will allow you to live your realistic fantasy. It is possible that your fantasy was different than you expected. What is crucial for the previous exercise to be successful is not to project what you *think* your fantasy is. For example, when I did this exercise after I moved away from my old life, I was expecting to fantasize about lots of money, the perfect home and the perfect business. But, when I removed all preconceptions and just allowed my fantasy to take over, here is what I wrote down, ***"Light pours into my body from the stars and expands like from within a diamond in all directions healing, enlightening and transforming the world."*** That was it. I won't lie to you. I was disappointed... at first. Then, I realized the genius of that concept. Because, now I was truly thinking shamanically. At first, that fantasy sounded nice, but the money, the house and the job were missing. You see, when I was previously projecting the money, house and other things into my fantasy, I was operating from a limited constraint that was derived from a feeling of need. Money, houses and other things are very nice and necessary, but they are extraneous details to our lives. Once you have the money and the house etc.., you still need to DO something. You need to LIVE. This is the goal of the shamanic fantasy; to find out what dream you will be LIVING when you have the stuff. So, start from the position that you already have all of the stuff. When you have it, you won't be spending time thinking about the house, you will be thinking about what to do. So, start the fantasy as though you already have it and are very happy. The one criticism I have with the modern idea of the "Law of Attraction" (it is actually a very old concept) is that people are using it as a means to attract "stuff." People pour all kinds of emotion into cars and houses etc... (I know I have.) Usually this works in the beginning, but then success in attracting their desires slowly fades and people end up more disappointed than before. I believe I know why. It is because the Law of Attraction is not about attracting physical things. It is about attracting spiritual things. If you believe it is necessary to have physical things in order to be able to live a spiritual life, then start your fantasy as though you already have all the stuff that you need. But, don't waste time imagining all the details of the stuff. Just begin from the standpoint that whatever it is you truly desire (whether you know what that stuff is or not) is already in your life. This way, you are not limiting yourself. Because, in my experience, we really don't know what we want and whatever fantasies we indulge in are usually far less than what we get if we are in the flow of Spirit. The shamanic wealth theory is this: If you are living your highest destiny, you will receive all the stuff your body needs in order to help you LIVE your spiritual destiny. So, the real fantasy exercise is to imagine that you already have all the physical things you need in order to free your spirit to soar. This is the real fantasy. Anyone can imagine lots of money, cars and a big house. But how many people do you know who fantasize about living their highest spiritual destiny. Many may say, "Of course I want to live a spiritual life, but first I need take care of my financial needs so I have the time and freedom to then live my spiritual destiny." This is how I once thought. It is perfectly understandable. In modern society, we have been taught that possessions, jobs and money are what is most important and that emotional and spiritual fulfillment are secondary. But, this is backwards thinking based on an outdated model. When I was a kid, the typical model for success in life was to go to school, decide on a career path before high school ended, graduate and either enter college, the military or a trade school. Then after secondary education, you found a job in your chosen field, worked at one job for 30 years and lived on your retirement savings. This model nowadays is the most successful recipe for failure. To succeed in today's economy, one must be prepared to change jobs frequently and be prepared to learn multiple trades and change careers at the drop of a hat. It would be pointless to try and achieve success in today's world using my parents' outdated methodology because it limits your ability to adapt to modern realities. Likewise, when we fantasize about our ideal life, if we focus on the spiritual goal, we open ourselves to adapt on a physical level. We will be able to spontaneously flow with Spirit. To do this properly, we will need to live by faith. I don't mean the old religious kind of faith that sits around waiting for God to bring us something. I mean the kind of faith that actively listens to our innermost spirit and has the courage to take whatever immediate action is necessary. This is the shamanic way. All creation has a spirit and can speak to us directly. By living in the flow of the Spirit, we are able to listen to what is needed in any moment.

I must at this point share what may be hard for some to hear. The world is changing. Time and Energy are flowing faster than ever before. If we cling to the river bank of materialism, we will be swept into the rocks. If we let go and flow with the stream, we will be in the midst of Life. Physical possessions will not bring security any longer. True wealth is different now than it was even in my lifetime. True wealth is being able to flow with every moment and change with the flow of time. We are already seeing this. I need not mention all the celebrities who have all the fame and money anyone could ever want who are absolutely miserable. Have you ever said to yourself, "If I had their money and success, I would know how to use it"? Why can't I have their money?" But, think about it. If their money, success and fame failed to make them happy, what makes you think that those possessions would not also destroy you? I predict that as we move further into the next age, we will see more and more celebrities who "have it all" begin to self-destruct. So, what we learn is that money and possessions don't give us the freedom to then live our spiritual destinies. Like our "primitive" fellow humans, we realize that everything is already here for us. There is only the task of living our highest destiny. Let me bring us back to my friend who lived on the beach with no possessions. When he relives that time of his life, you can see his whole face change. He exudes a peacefulness that few have known. Now, I am saying that part of his happiness is due to his point of view. Someone else could have been in the same position as he was then and feel as though they were a homeless loser. But because my friend was "on vacation" this allowed him to feel that it was OK for him to be broke, homeless and jobless. For a local villager, the idea of being broke, homeless and living in a hammock may have changed his mindset into being a homeless loser. The difference between a homeless loser and a man with endless bounty and no responsibilities is simply one's mindset. That same friend after 6 months of living in paradise, came back home to the "real world" and got a job, a wife, kids, mortgage etc... He was not so happy anymore. He left his shamanic understanding of abundance and exchanged it for the modern idea of responsibility. While he was on the beach, even though he was "slacking off" and living his selfish dream. He was providing villagers with fish. His dream of spending his days spear-fishing not only gave him great satisfaction, but also provided food for those around him. We have been told a lie that we cannot be productive and be deliriously happy at the same time. The shamanic viewpoint is that our destiny is to live our wildest dreams and the result will be that we provide services for others. Productivity and usefulness is the result of spiritual living. The difference for my friend was that while he was on that tropical beach, he knew that everything he needed was there all around him. He lived simply because he believed that he needed very little. And he was right. He knew that the ocean would supply him everyday with food and with whatever fish he had left over he could trade with the local villagers for rice, beans, vegetables, clothes and other supplies. The only things he needed were his tent, hammock and spear gun. Nature would provide everything else he needed.

So, now we are ready for the actual shamanic fantasy exercise…
However, I must be truthful and tell you. You already did it. The warm-up was the real exercise. I lied and told you it was only a warm-up so you would not project a more "responsible" version into your brain. As I said earlier, this is my main criticism of the current version of the "law of attraction." As is proven by modern society, possessions are not true wealth. Our fulfillment comes from living our deepest fantasies. These fantasies are always of a spiritual nature. Fantasies of being superman or batman or Joan of Arc or whatever fantasies that bring you the deepest sense of joy and adventure are what your spirit yearns for. Maybe you will be superman, maybe something more down-to earth. I don't know. I do know that we are here for one purpose, to evolve and help all of creation to evolve with us. There is no higher calling. While all of us fantasize of this when we are children, most of us grow up to accept the "responsible" realities fed to us by our society.

I once had a very elaborate fantasy of my perfect life which included details about a house and career, but I now see that my original warm-up exercise fantasy of being filled with a celestial light that flows to all things in the Universe and aids in its evolution is my highest calling and my deepest source of fulfillment. And, the great thing is, along the way, I get the fantasy house, career and relationship because these are things that I need to fulfill my spiritual destiny as a practicing shaman in the modern world.

The next usual step in these kinds of books is to go into detail about how to set goals and achieve them. I will leave those kinds of instructions to those who have already written the many practical books on such things. In my experience, Learning how to set goals etc.. are pointless if you do not know who you are and why you are here. Find that out first and then learn the practical goal setting exercises. But, if you are truly excited about your goal, you will have little problem going after it. My suggestion is to investigate other shamanic practices to help you use spirit power to achieve your highest destiny. I have made many other sources of shamanic spiritual tools available such as books, CDs, DVDs, streaming videos and live teachings. There are so many spiritual and energetic tools available out there that I can assure you that if you do this, you won't have time to worry about physical possessions. The Universe will bring everything you need because you will be actively fulfilling your spiritual purpose, which is sorely needed in this crucial time we live in.

Thank you for taking the time to read this short book. You may be thinking that this book is too short. I wrote this book to be short for a reason. It doesn't need to be longer. I would rather you take the time that you would have spent reading a three hundred page book and use that time to practice and meditate on the previous exercises. Sometimes quantity is not quality. This is the case with this subject. The exercises I have laid out in this book can take a lifetime to perfect and understand. I know that the typical formula for a self-help book is to fill it with hundreds of pages of stories and exercises. I won't lie to you. I strongly felt the temptation to do the same here. I am a pretty smart guy and I could have easily filled this book with hundreds of pages of exercises and info. And it all would have been relevant and no doubt interesting. But the real teaching is in the pages I have already written here. If I continued to fill pages with words in order to fit some preconceived stereotype of what a self-help book is, the real teaching would become diluted.

Please do not be discouraged if you do not see the results you expected right away. Mental resistance is the biggest hurdle to seeing clearly our shamanic truths and manifesting them. Everyone is different. There is such a thing as Karma. If you have grown up in stifling or abusive homes as children, there is a very good chance that you may have created a lot of mental and emotional armor in order to protect yourself. This is why I always recommend counseling. I myself have been in some form of counseling for the past thirty years. I have no intention of changing that practice. We need objective outside help. This was another aspect of shamanic living that our ancestors practiced. The family and tribal unit was very important. In those days, the elders were always available to advise us. In modern society, we have lost that inherent support system. However, we humans have not changed very much in the past two thousand years of modern "civilization." We are still biologically designed to function in a spiritual community and solve problems shamanically. Well, it is a fact that tribal unit has disappeared, so we need to be proactive and fill that need with what we have. In times past, we sought out the tribal shaman to gain objective advice. Today, we seek out counselors and teachers. For those wishing further counseling, please seek it out from whatever source you are drawn to. I am available on a limited basis for private counseling as well.

Why This Stuff Works

This chapter is specifically for those individuals who might be new shamanic thinking. This stuff may sound very simplistic or even childish. Your intellect may be having a real hard time swallowing that things like poverty and prosperity have consciousness and run around outside of us acting on their own volition. I completely understand and sympathize with your dilemma. And I want to tell you that it doesn't really matter. In other words, it's OK to have all the doubts in the world. If you simply follow these simple guidelines and do the exercises regardless of your beliefs, you will see results. Why?

Well, first off, this is not religion. You don't have to have faith for it to work. Shamanic principles are very powerful psychological tools. Those of you familiar with psychology, hypnosis, NLP, etc, will see what I am saying. These principles cut right to the core of our subconscious where most of our psychological patterns are stored. I was once told that 99% of all our actions stem from our subconscious and unconscious psychological patterns. We think we know why we do what we do, but in reality, our conscious mind has no idea why we do what we do. Our conscious mind is just along for the ride and we tell ourselves little stories to justify our actions. But, the reality is that we are totally clueless.

One of my students told me a story that illustrates this principle very well. He told me that he had read about a psychological study involving people whose corpus collossum had been damaged. (The corpus collossum is the small section of brain tissue that connects the two hemispheres of the brain and allows the right hemisphere to communicate with the left hemisphere of the brain.) In one instance, the patient was given a command in only one ear, which would mean that since the patient did not have a corpus collussum that only one side of the brain would hear the command. The patient was told to "stand up and walk across the room." The patient did so. Then in the other ear, the patient was asked, "Why did you get up just now?" To which the patient responded, "I wanted to get a drink of water." This was a total lie! If I remember the conclusion of that particular incident, it meant that the left brain had invented a completely false reason for why the body got up and walked across the room. In other words, the patient thought he knew exactly why he was doing what he was doing but the truth is that he had no clue, but in order to keep his perception of reality intact, his brain concocted a totally false reality for him having to do with being thirsty.

Another study I read about had to with the study of how decisions were registered in the brain. Electrodes were hooked up to peoples' heads and electrical impulses were recorded. The patients were asked to do small things like pick up a pencil, push a button, etc... The hypothesis of the study was that when the decision to pick up the pencil was made, it would show up as an electrical impulse in the brain milliseconds before the action was taken. Well, the results totally mystified the scientists. What they found is that the brain only registered electrical impulses in the brain AFTER the action had been taken. If their theory is correct, that would mean that decisions aren't even made in the brain at all. The brain only records the action afterwards and then tries to justify the action after the fact.

What does this mean for us? In modern society we try to intellectually understand everything including abstract concepts like poverty and prosperity. Based on those two studies and my own personal experience, I believe that the intellect is very bad at figuring things out on an abstract level. So, in the case of prosperity, using the intellect to try and understand an energetic, spiritual or even psychological issue is like trying to look at an Elephant through a microscope. You could spend your whole life trying to piece together the whole picture of an elephant and still have no idea what you are looking at.
Human beings have been animists and shamans for hundreds of thousands of years. It has only been in the last few hundred years that we have become "rational thinkers." For thousands and thousands of years our ancestors communicated directly with the spirit of things.

Why is this important?
Well, let's just assume for argument's sake that prosperity might not be as I have described it here. I still say that treating it like it has its own consciousness and spirit is the best way to understand and work with Her. Why? Because, the human species has evolved this method of problem solving over millions of years. We are evolved for shamanism. Birds have evolved wings for flight, fish have evolved gills for breathing under water and human beings have evolved shamanic thought processes for problem solving. So, even if what I am saying were not true, (which of course, I believe it IS true), it is still in our best interest to use the tools that we have honed over millions of years of evolution for our survival. Shamanic thought and techniques are not primitive superstitions, they are profound and complex problem solving skills that have allowed the human race to become the dominant species on the planet. By re-awakening that which is already part of our inherent nature is the most logical and most efficient way to survive.
So, even if you don't rationally believe some of the things I have written here, I think you will find that if you simply "act as if," you may find that

it will result in powerful results for you because that is what you have been pre-wired to do. And the more you practice it, the better you will become at doing it and the better results you will get.

If you want to further empower your shamanic vision, please look at these websites:
General Spiritual Tools for transformation:
www.TheHolographicMind.com
Mantra and sacred Sound: www.SecretWordsofPower.com
Qigong and Taoist Meditation: www.SpiritTao.com
Modern Western Shamanism: www.ThunderWizard.com

May you be blessed by the
spirits of abundant
prosperity and spiritual
fulfillment....

Made in the USA
Monee, IL
23 April 2022

95263615R00020